Food Chains

by Grace Hansen

BEGINNING SCIENCE: ECOLOGY

Abdo Kids Jumbo is an Imprint of Abdo Kids
abdobooks.com

abdobooks.com

Published by Abdo Kids, a division of ABDO, P.O. Box 398166, Minneapolis, Minnesota 55439.
Copyright © 2020 by Abdo Consulting Group, Inc. International copyrights reserved in all countries.
No part of this book may be reproduced in any form without written permission from the publisher.
Abdo Kids Jumbo™ is a trademark and logo of Abdo Kids.

Printed in the United States of America, North Mankato, Minnesota.

102019

012020

THIS BOOK CONTAINS
RECYCLED MATERIALS

Photo Credits: iStock, Shutterstock

Production Contributors: Teddy Borth, Jennie Forsberg, Grace Hansen
Design Contributors: Dorothy Toth, Pakou Moua

Library of Congress Control Number: 2019941228
Publisher's Cataloging-in-Publication Data

Names: Hansen, Grace, author.

Title: Food chains / by Grace Hansen

Description: Minneapolis, Minnesota : Abdo Kids, 2020 | Series: Beginning science: ecology |
    Includes online resources and index.

Identifiers: ISBN 9781532188947 (lib. bdg.) | ISBN 9781644942673 (pbk.) |
    ISBN 9781532189432 (ebook) | ISBN 9781098200411 (Read-to-Me ebook)

Subjects: LCSH: Food chains (Ecology)--Juvenile literature. | Nutrient cycles--Juvenile literature. | Food
    webs (Ecology)--Juvenile literature. | Ecology--Juvenile literature. | Food supply--Juvenile literature.

Classification: DDC 577.16--dc23

Table of Contents

What Is a Food Chain? 4

Producers 10

Consumers 12

Let's Review! 22

Glossary 23

Index 24

Abdo Kids Code. 24

What Is a Food Chain?

A food chain shows how energy moves through an **ecosystem**.

All the energy in a food chain begins with the sun. Plants get energy from sunlight.

Plants turn sunlight into chemical energy. This is a process called photosynthesis.

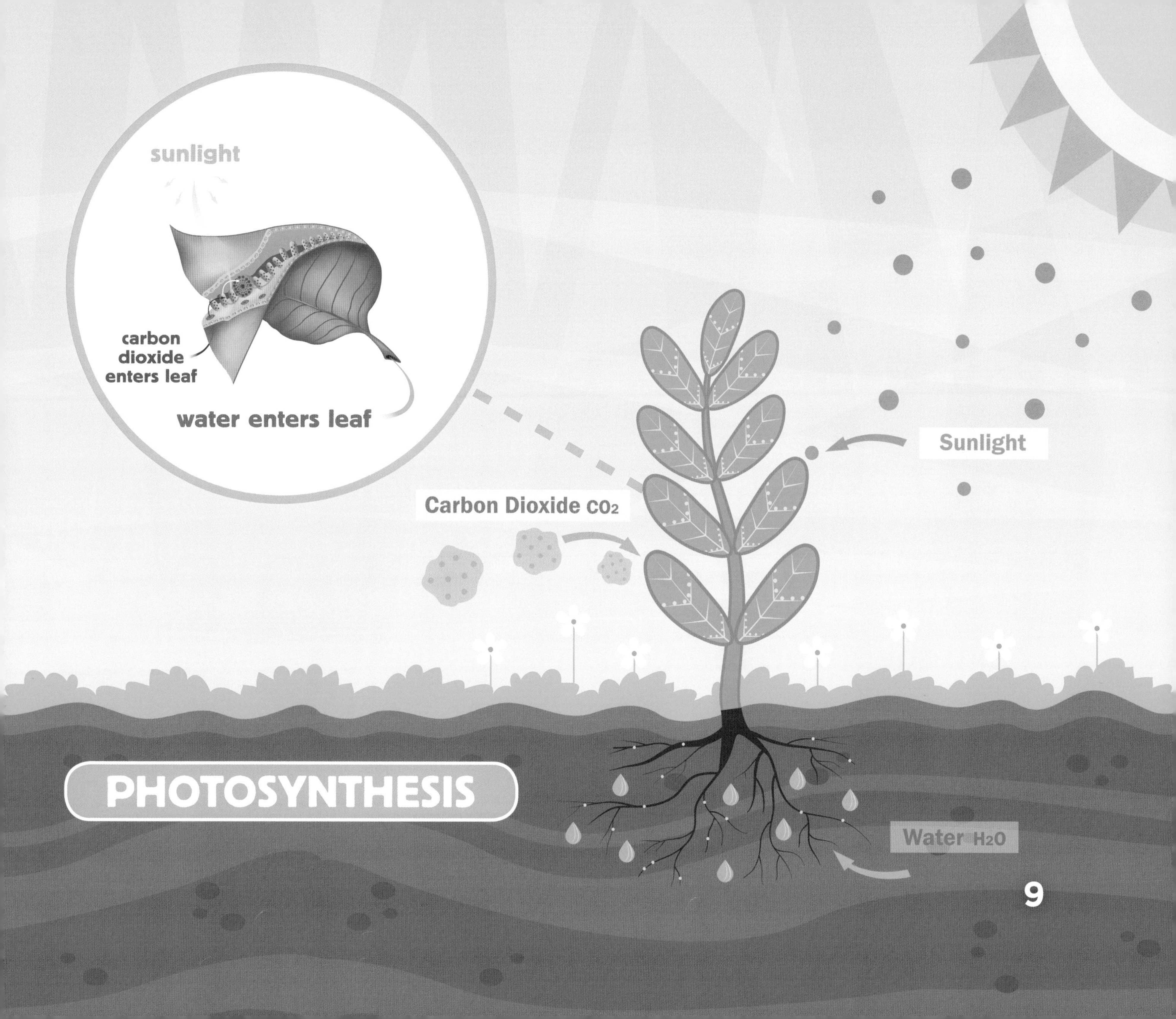

sunlight

carbon
dioxide
enters leaf

water enters leaf

Sunlight

Carbon Dioxide CO_2

Water H_2O

PHOTOSYNTHESIS

9

Producers

In the food chain, plants are called primary producers. They make their own food.

11

Consumers

Consumers cannot make their own food. Unlike plants, they must eat something else to get energy.

13

Animals that only eat plants are called herbivores. In the food chain, they are called primary consumers. Giraffes and sheep eat only plants.

Secondary consumers include

omnivores and carnivores.

Omnivores eat plants and meat.

Bears eat berries and fish.

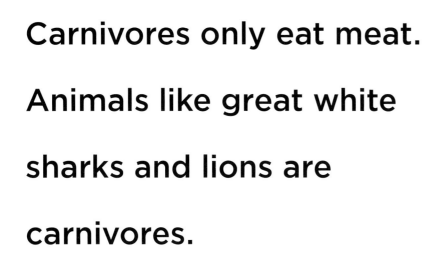

Carnivores only eat meat. Animals like great white sharks and lions are carnivores.

Decomposers and **detritivores** are special kinds of consumers. They break down waste. This puts nutrients back into soil, which helps plants grow. The cycle begins again!

Let's Review!

- A food chain shows how energy flows through an ecosystem.

- Plants make their own food using sunlight.

- An herbivore eats plants. The energy from the plants transfers to it.

- The energy transfers again when another animal eats the herbivore.

- Scavengers and detritivores eat dead plants and animals, or animal droppings for energy. Decomposers break down the leftover waste.

22

Glossary

decomposer – an organism, like bacteria or fungus, that breaks down dead, organic matter in the environment, sometimes after a scavenger is done with it.

detritivore – a type of decomposer that eats dead, organic matter and digests it internally to gain nutrients.

ecosystem – a community of livings things, together with their environment.

Index

carnivore 16, 18

consumers 12, 14, 16, 20

decomposers 20

detritivores 20

herbivore 14

omnivore 16

photosynthesis 8

plants 6, 8, 10, 12, 14, 16, 20

primary consumers 14

primary producers 10

secondary consumers 16

sun 6, 8

Abdo Kids
ONLINE
FREE! ONLINE MULTIMEDIA RESOURCES

Visit **abdokids.com** to access crafts, games, videos, and more!

Use Abdo Kids code

BFK8947

or scan this QR code!